50 IN 50

THE FIFTY SELF-HELP MASTERPIECES: A CONCISE SUMMARY COMPILATION

INKWELL NOMAD

"I dedicate "50 in 50" to all the seekers of self-improvement and personal growth. To those who strive to be the best version of themselves, who never stop learning and growing. To those who are willing to put in the hard work and dedication to achieve their goals and dreams. This book is for you."

Contents

Contents

Preface

"Welcome to "50 in 50." This book is the culmination of years of research and study in the field of personal development. I, Inkwell Nomad, have always been passionate about self-improvement and have spent countless hours reading and analyzing the works of the world's top self-help authors.

In this book, I have distilled the key takeaways and lessons of some of the most popular and influential self-help books into a concise and easy-to-read format. This is not a replacement for reading the original books, but rather, a way to quickly gain valuable insights and wisdom from them.

I believe that everyone can benefit from the wisdom contained in these books, regardless of their background or experience level. Whether you're a busy professional looking to improve your productivity, a student seeking to boost your confidence, or a parent looking to strengthen your relationships, this book has something for you.

I have selected the books in various categories, making it easy for you to find the information you're looking for. Each summary includes key takeaways and actionable advice that you can implement in your life right away.

I hope that this book will serve as a valuable resource for you on your journey of personal growth and self-improvement. Thank you for taking the time to read it. "

P.S: This book is in no way a substitute for the 50 books browsed but a glimpse to motivate the readers to find their path and explore further. I recommend to read one book per day at max. and reflect on it.

Acknowledgements

With love and gratitude to my Spouse & Daughter...!

Thanks to the authors of these 50 self-help books that have transformed millions of lives and yet more to be transformed...!

CHAPTER I

Atomic Habits – James Clear

This book focuses on the small changes that can lead to big results over time. Clear argues that small, consistent changes in behavior, or atomic habits, can add up to significant progress and improvement. The book covers the four laws of behavior change, viz: 'it' refers to new habits.

1. Make it obvious: This could include setting reminders, placing items in an easy visible location or making a list of your habits.
2. Make it attractive: This could include visualizing the benefits of the new habit or finding a way to make the habit enjoyable.
3. Make it easy: This could include breaking the habit down into smaller steps or finding ways to automate it.
4. Make it satisfying: This could include celebrating your progress, finding a way to make the habit enjoyable or rewarding yourself for sticking to it.

Clear also suggests below techniques to reinforce the habits and transform your life,

1. Start small: Clear suggests that small changes can lead to big results over time, so it's important to start with small, manageable habits rather than trying to make big changes all at once.
2. Create a system: Clear suggests that you create a system for habit change, rather than relying on willpower alone. This could include setting up triggers and rewards, tracking your progress or finding an accountability partner.
3. Understand the identity level of habits: Clear suggests that you understand the underlying reasons why you want to change a habit, and create a belief system that aligns with your desired habits.
4. Use the "Two-Minute Rule": Clear suggests that you use the "Two-Minute Rule" which states that making it easy to get started is more important than making it perfect.

CHAPTER II

7 Habits of Highly Effective People – Stephen R. Covey

The book emphasizes on the "Inside-Out Approach" which means that true effectiveness comes from the alignment of one's values and principles with one's actions and habits. The seven habits essential to be effective are as below and followed by some tips to stick the habits:

1. Being Proactive: taking initiative and responsibility for one's actions.
2. Starting with the end in mind: having clear goals & a plan to achieve them.
3. Putting first things first: prioritizing important tasks over less important ones.
4. Thinking win-win: seeking mutually beneficial solutions in relationships and interactions.
5. Seeking first to understand, then to be understood: Listening actively and empathizing with others before communicating one's own perspective.
6. Synergizing: working effectively with others to achieve common goals.
7. Sharpening the saw: continuously improving and balancing one's physical, emotional, mental, & spiritual well-being.

Create a personal mission statement that defines your purpose and goals in life concisely and clearly. Use time management tools and techniques to prioritize e.g. Practice the "ABCDE" method: Prioritize tasks by identifying the most important ones (A tasks) and work on them first, before moving on to less important tasks (B and C). Practice active listening and empathy to understand others before communicating your own perspective. Use the "5 Whys" technique to get to the root cause of any problem. Find an accountability partner to provide support and motivation. Keep a journal as a tool to reflect on your progress and to track your habits. Take regular breaks to avoid burnout and to give your mind a chance to recharge.

CHAPTER III

The Four Agreements – Don Miguel Ruiz

The book presents a simple but powerful code of conduct for attaining personal freedom and true happiness.

- The first agreement is "Be Impeccable with Your Word." This means to speak with integrity and to avoid using the word to speak against yourself or to gossip about others.
- The second agreement is "Don't Take Anything Personally." This means that what others say or do is a projection of their own reality, and has nothing to do with you.
- The third agreement is "Don't Make Assumptions." This means to communicate clearly and ask for what you want, rather than making assumptions about what others are thinking or feeling.
- The fourth agreement is "Always Do Your Best." This means to strive for excellence in all that you do, and to understand that your best will change from moment to moment, depending on your energy level and external circumstances.

The book also includes a fifth agreement, "Be skeptical, but learn to listen", which means to question everything, but also to keep an open mind and be willing to learn from others.

The book argues that by living these agreements, one can break free from the emotional prison of self-limiting beliefs and societal conditioning. The Four Agreements offer a powerful code of conduct that can rapidly transform one's life to a new experience of freedom, true happiness, and love.

CHAPTER IV

Man's Search for Meaning – Viktor E. Frankl

This book was written by Viktor Frankl, a Holocaust survivor, in which he describes his experiences in Nazi concentration camps during World War II and his observations on the human search for meaning in life. The book is divided into two parts: the first describes Frankl's experiences in the camps, and the second describes his theory of logotherapy, which is based on the idea that people's primary drive in life is not pleasure, but the search for meaning and purpose.

1. Finding meaning in suffering: Frankl argues that even in the most dire circumstances, such as those he faced in the concentration camps, people can find meaning and purpose in their lives, and that this is essential for survival. He suggests that individuals should focus on finding meaning in their suffering, rather than just trying to escape or avoid it.

2. The importance of self-transcendence: Frankl suggests that people should strive to transcend their own personal interests and focus on something greater than themselves. This could be a cause, a person, or a goal that is meaningful to them.

3. The power of attitude: Frankl observed that those who had a positive attitude and a sense of purpose were more likely to survive the concentration camps. He emphasizes the importance of maintaining a positive attitude in the face of adversity and focusing on the things that one can control.

4. The value of personal responsibility: Frankl suggests that people should take personal responsibility for their actions and reactions in life. He believes that individuals can choose their attitude towards a situation, and that this choice can have a significant impact on how they experience it.

5. The need for relationships: Frankl observed that human beings have a deep need for relationships and connections with others. He suggests that people should strive to build meaningful relationships and connections with others, as they can provide a sense of support, purpose, and meaning in life.

CHAPTER V

Awaken the Giant Within – Tony Robbins

This book aims to help readers take control of their lives and achieve their goals. The book covers a wide range of topics, including personal finance, career development, relationships, and personal growth. Robbins emphasizes the importance of taking action and making changes in order to achieve success. He also encourages readers to identify and overcome limiting beliefs and to set clear, measurable goals.

Some tips from Tony Robbins:

- Take control of your emotions: Robbins argues that our emotions are not something that happen to us, but rather something that we create. He encourages readers to take control of their emotions by identifying and changing their thoughts and beliefs.
- Set clear and measurable goals: Robbins emphasizes the importance of setting clear, measurable goals in order to achieve success. He suggests breaking down larger goals into smaller, more manageable steps.
- Take massive action: Robbins encourages readers to take massive action in order to achieve their goals. He argues that taking action is more important than having a perfect plan.
- Identify and overcome limiting beliefs: Robbins suggests that many of our problems stem from limiting beliefs that we hold about ourselves. He encourages readers to identify these beliefs and to take steps to overcome them.
- Develop a powerful self-image: Robbins believes that the way we see ourselves shapes our actions and our results. He encourages readers to develop a powerful self-image by focusing on their strengths and accomplishments.
- Master the art of persuasion: Robbins emphasizes the importance of persuasion in achieving success. He teaches readers how to communicate effectively and to influence others to achieve their goals.
- Create a compelling future: Robbins encourages readers to create a vivid, compelling vision of the future they want to achieve. He suggests that this can help to motivate and inspire them to take action.

CHAPTER VI

Daring Greatly – Brené Brown

The book is about the power of vulnerability and how it relates to shame and fear of judgment. The author argues that vulnerability is the core of shame, fear, and our struggle for worthiness, but it is also the birthplace of joy, belonging, creativity, and love. The author claims that vulnerability is the key to living a wholehearted life, where we can embrace our imperfections, and believe that we are worthy of love and belonging.

The book's main message is that when we dare greatly, we open ourselves up to the possibility of both hurt and reward.

Brené Brown offers several tips for embracing vulnerability and living a wholehearted life:

1. Recognize and understand the impact of shame and fear on your life. Vulnerability is not the absence of fear, but the ability to move through fear, and that the only way to be vulnerable is to be honest about our fears

2. Embrace vulnerability as a strength. Recognize that vulnerability is not weakness, but rather the courage to show up and be seen.

3. Practice self-compassion and self-kindness. Be gentle with yourself and understand that you are worthy of love and belonging.

4. Learn to move through fear. Understand that vulnerability involves risk, but it is a risk that is well worth taking.

5. Build trust through vulnerability. Understand that vulnerability is the only path to true connection and intimacy.

6. Practice gratitude and joy. Focus on the good in your life, and actively practice gratitude and joy.

7. Cultivate a sense of belonging. Understand that we are all connected and that we all need a sense of belonging in order to thrive.

8. Speak the truth with kindness. Learn to communicate openly and honestly, while also being kind and respectful to others.

9. Practice self-care. Take care of yourself physically, emotionally, and spiritually, in order to be able to show up and be vulnerable.

CHAPTER VII

The Gifts of Imperfection – Brené Brown

The book encourages readers to embrace their vulnerabilities and imperfections in order to live a more authentic and fulfilling life. Brown argues that by embracing vulnerability and imperfection, individuals can build deeper connections with others and find greater self-acceptance. She also discusses the importance of letting go of societal expectations and the need for perfection, in order to lead a more authentic and meaningful life. Overall, the book aims to help readers develop a greater sense of self-compassion and self-worth, and to live a more authentic and fulfilling life.

1. Cultivate authenticity: Allow yourself to be vulnerable and be true to yourself, rather than trying to meet societal expectations or fit into a certain mold.
2. Practice self-compassion: Be kind and understanding towards yourself, rather than criticizing and judging yourself for your imperfections.
3. Let go of perfectionism: Recognize that perfection is unattainable and that it is okay to make mistakes and be imperfect.
4. Connect with others: Share your vulnerabilities with others and build deeper, more authentic relationships.
5. Cultivate gratitude and joy: Practice being grateful for what you have and find joy in the present moment.
6. Cultivate a strong sense of self-worth: Recognize that you are worthy of love and belonging, regardless of your imperfections.
7. Find meaning in your values: Identify your values and use them to guide your actions and decision-making.
8. Practice mindfulness: Be present and aware in the moment, rather than dwelling on the past or worrying about the future.
9. Embrace your imperfections: Accept and love yourself, flaws and all.
10. Take action: Apply these principles in your daily life, and make a conscious effort to cultivate authenticity, self-compassion, and self-worth.

CHAPTER VIII

How to Stop Worrying and Start Living – Dale Carnegie

Carnegie argues that worry is a habit that can be broken by learning to focus on the present moment and taking action to solve problems. He also emphasizes the importance of developing a positive attitude and learning to view problems as opportunities for growth. Throughout the book, Carnegie provides a variety of tools and strategies for managing worry, such as visualization, affirmations, and time management.

- Live in the present moment: Focus on the present and take action to solve problems, rather than dwelling on the past or worrying about the future.
- Practice positive self-talk: Replace negative thoughts with positive affirmations and statements.
- Use visualization: Imagine yourself successfully dealing with a problem or achieving a goal in detail.
- Prioritize your worries: Identify the most important and urgent worries and deal with them first.
- Keep a worry period: Set aside a specific time each day to write down and think about your worries, this will help you to tackle them more effectively.
- Practice gratitude: Be thankful for what you have and focus on the blessings in your life.
- Learn to let go: Let go of past mistakes and regrets, and focus on moving forward.
- Develop a positive attitude: Look for the good in situations, rather than dwelling on the negative.
- Take action: Take small steps towards solving problems and achieving goals, and don't be afraid to take risks.
- Seek support: Talk to someone you trust about your worries, this will help you to put things in perspective and find solutions.

CHAPTER IX

The Magic of Thinking Big – David J Schwartz

"The Magic of Thinking Big" by David J. Schwartz offers insights and practical tips on how to achieve success through positive thinking and goal setting.

Anecdote: The author shares a story about a man who started a small business and was facing difficulty in growing it. He attended a lecture by the author, applied the principles of positive thinking, and soon his business took off, becoming one of the largest in his industry.

Summary: The book argues that having a positive mindset and setting big, challenging goals is the key to success. It emphasizes the importance of believing in oneself, surrounding oneself with positive influences, and taking action towards one's goals. The author also discusses the power of positive self-talk, visualization, and expanding one's thinking to maximize potential. The book suggests that people should not be afraid of failure, as it is a natural part of the learning process. It also encourages people to visualize their desired outcome and to think positively about it.

Some tips and takeaways from the book:

- Believe in yourself and your abilities.
- Set specific, measurable, and achievable goals.
- Surround yourself with positive, successful people.
- Take action towards your goals and persist despite setbacks.
- Practice positive self-talk and visualization.
- Expand your thinking to maximize your potential.

Overall, the book encourages readers to adopt a growth mindset and adopt the habits of successful people to achieve their full potential and attain great success in life.

CHAPTER X

The Power of Positive Thinking – Norman Vincent Peale

The book encourages readers to adopt a positive outlook on life in order to achieve success and overcome obstacles. Peale argues that by replacing negative thoughts with positive ones, individuals can improve their emotional and physical well-being, as well as their relationships and career prospects. He also discusses the importance of faith and prayer in achieving a positive mindset, and provides various techniques and exercises for developing a positive attitude, such as visualization and affirmations.

1. Affirmations: Repeat positive affirmations to yourself, such as "I am confident and capable" or "I am worthy of love and success."
2. Visualization: Imagine yourself successfully achieving your goals and visualize the details of what that would look like.
3. Reframing: Reframe negative thoughts and situations in a positive light, for example instead of thinking "I'll never be able to do this" think "I can do this, and I will find a way."
4. Gratitude: Practice being thankful for what you have and focus on the blessings in your life.
5. Faith: Believe in yourself and in a higher power to guide you.
6. Prayer: Use prayer as a way to focus your thoughts, release negative emotions and cultivate inner peace.
7. Action: Take small steps towards achieving your goals, and don't be afraid to take risks.
8. Forgiveness: Let go of grudges and resentments in order to move forward positively.
9. Surround yourself with positive influences: Seek out people who have a positive attitude and who will support your goals.
10. Resilience: When facing challenges, remember that difficulties are temporary and that you have the power to overcome them.

CHAPTER XI

Influence: The Psychology of Persuasion – Robert Cialdini

The book explores the psychological and social factors that influence human behavior and decision making. The book is divided into several chapters, each focused on a different principle of persuasion. Cialdini identifies six main principles: reciprocation, commitment and consistency, social proof, authority, liking, and scarcity.

- The principle of reciprocation states that people feel obligated to return a favor or a gift. This can be used to create a sense of indebtedness and influence people to do something in return.
- The principle of commitment and consistency states that people are more likely to do something if they have already made a commitment to do it. This is why people are more likely to follow through with something if they have publicly committed to it.
- The principle of social proof states that people are more likely to do something if they see others doing it. This is why people are more likely to buy a product if they see others buying it.
- The principle of authority states that people are more likely to do something if they perceive the person requesting it as an authority figure.
- The principle of liking states that people are more likely to do something if they like the person requesting it.
- The principle of scarcity states that people are more likely to want something if they believe it is scarce. This is why people are more likely to buy something if they believe it is in limited supply.

Throughout the book, Cialdini provides examples and research to illustrate the application of these principles in everyday life, as well as in advertising and sales, politics, and other areas. The book is considered a classic in the field of social psychology and has been widely read and studied for its insights into the nature of persuasion and human behavior.

CHAPTER XII

Predictably Irrational – Dan Ariely

This book is about the psychology of human decision-making and behavior. It explores the various factors that influence people's behavior and decision-making, and argues that people's behavior is often irrational, but predictable and explainable. The book provides insights into how these irrational behaviors can be influenced by the way choices are presented, and how they can be influenced by the emotions and feelings that are associated with them. To make more rational decisions,

- Understand the power of context in which decisions are made and how it can influence behavior.
- Be aware of emotions in decision-making and how they can lead to irrational behavior.
- Avoid the sunk cost fallacy which is the tendency to continue investing in a decision or action because of the resources that have already been invested, rather than evaluating if it makes sense to continue.
- Be mindful of the anchoring effect which is the tendency for people to rely too heavily on the first piece of information encountered when making decisions.
- Be aware of the endowment effect which is the tendency for people to value things more highly simply because they own them.
- The "decoy" effect: People's preferences can be manipulated by presenting them with a "decoy" option that makes the other options seem more or less attractive in comparison.
- Be aware of social norms in shaping behavior: People are more likely to engage in prosocial behavior (like donating to charity) when they see that others like them are doing the same.
- Be aware of the influence of price - the "zero price effect": People tend to place a higher value on things that are free, even if they have no use for them.
- Be aware of the influence of time - the "present bias" effect: Ariely demonstrates how people tend to give more weight to the present and the immediate future, and less weight to the future. E.g. One would rather take $100 now than to wait for $150 next month.

CHAPTER XIII

Thinking Fast and Slow – Daniel Kahneman

This book explores the psychology of decision making, and how our mind works when we think. The brain has an estimated 100 billion neurons, each of which can make thousands of connections with other neurons. How these connections give rise to thoughts, memories, and behaviors is still not fully understood.

One of the biggest mysteries of the human brain is how it creates consciousness. Scientists are still trying to understand how the brain's neural activity gives rise to subjective experiences such as thoughts, emotions, and perceptions.

The book is divided into two systems of thinking: "System 1" which is fast, intuitive, and emotional, and "System 2" which is slow, deliberate, and logical. In summary, "Thinking, Fast and Slow" argues that our mind is often influenced by cognitive biases and heuristics, which can lead to irrational decisions. Some of the key insights from the book are:

Our mind is wired to make quick judgments based on the information available to us, this is known as System 1 thinking.

System 1 thinking is prone to errors and biases, such as the availability heuristic (the tendency to overestimate the probability of rare events) and the sunk cost fallacy (the tendency to continue investing in a decision because of previous investments).

System 2 thinking is a slower, more deliberate process that can help us overcome these biases and make more rational decisions.

Kahneman also discusses the concept of "loss aversion," the idea that people feel the pain of losses more than the pleasure of gains. An external account notes that to compensate each unit of loss, one must gain 2.8x - E.g. If I lose $100, it will take $280 to compensate my feeling of loss.

He also describes the concept of "anchoring," the idea that people's judgments are influenced by an initial value or starting point, and the "framing effect," the idea that people's decisions can be influenced by how a problem or choice is presented to them.

Overall, the book provides a detailed account of how our mind works and how to avoid common cognitive biases, helping to make better decisions.

CHAPTER XIV

Deep Work – Cal Newport

Newport argues that the ability to focus and perform deep, meaningful work is becoming increasingly valuable in today's economy. The author defines deep work as long stretches of focused, distraction-free work and presents the idea that it is the key to achieving success in today's economy. He states that deep work can be learned and improved through practice and by developing a set of habits and rituals that help to enable focus.

1. Schedule time for deep work: Set specific times during the day when you'll engage in deep work, and stick to that schedule as closely as possible.
2. Eliminate distractions: Create an environment that is conducive to deep work by eliminating distractions, such as social media, email, and notifications.
3. Use the Pomodoro Technique: Break your deep work sessions into smaller chunks of time, such as 25 minutes of focused work followed by a 5-minute break.
4. Prioritize deep work over shallow tasks: Identify the most important tasks that require deep focus and prioritize them over less important, shallow tasks.
5. Find your optimal environment for deep work: Experiment with different environments to find the one that allows you to focus the best
6. Learn to embrace boredom: Learn to tolerate boredom and discomfort when working on hard tasks, as this is often a sign that you're engaged in deep work.
7. Practice mindfulness: Be present and focused in the moment in order to eliminate distractions and increase focus.
8. Avoid multitasking: Avoid multitasking and focus on one task at a time in order to achieve a deeper level of focus.
9. Embrace your solitude: Use your alone time to engage in deep work and avoid socializing during deep work sessions.
10. Take breaks: Regularly take breaks to avoid burnout, and to give your mind a chance to recharge.

CHAPTER XV

The Compound Effect – Darren Hardy

The book presents the idea that small, consistent actions lead to significant results over time. Hardy argues that success is not the result of one big decision or action, but rather the cumulative effect of many small decisions and actions. He also emphasizes the importance of having a clear vision and setting specific goals, and provides practical strategies for developing the habits and routines that are necessary for achieving success. Hardy also encourages readers to focus on the long-term and to be patient with the process of achieving their goals. The book contains a lot of examples to illustrate the ideas. Tips and techniques:

- Start small: Take small, consistent actions towards achieving your goals and let the compound effect take over.
- Set Specific Goals: Clearly define your goals and create a plan to achieve them.
- Track your progress: Keep track of your progress and measure your results to stay motivated.
- Focus on the long-term: Keep your eye on the bigger picture and be patient with the process of achieving your goals.
- Build good habits: Develop good habits that support your goals, and eliminate those that don't.
- Eliminate bad habits: Identify and eliminate bad habits that are holding you back from achieving your goals.
- Surround yourself with positive influences: Seek out people who have a positive attitude and who will support your goals.
- Stay consistent: Consistency is key, make sure to take consistent actions towards achieving your goals.
- Learn from failure: Learn from your failures and use them as opportunities for growth.
- Stay flexible: Be open to change and be willing to adjust your plan if necessary.

CHAPTER XVI

The ONE Thing – Gary Keller

The book is a guide to achieving success by focusing on one important goal at a time through a simplified mental process.

- Identify your "One Thing": The book encourages readers to identify their most important goal and to focus all their efforts on it. It suggests that by focusing on one thing at a time, people can achieve more than they ever thought possible.
- Eliminate distractions: The book encourages readers to simplify their lives by eliminating distractions and unnecessary activities. It suggests that by eliminating distractions, people can focus their attention on their "One Thing" and achieve it more quickly.
- Set priorities: The book stresses the importance of time management and the power of setting priorities. By focusing on one task or goal at a time, rather than trying to do too many things at once, people can achieve more.
- Take consistent action: The book encourages readers to take consistent action towards their goal and to create a system to achieve it. It suggests that by taking consistent action, people can achieve more than they ever thought possible.
- Track progress: The book encourages readers to find a way to measure their progress and to track their results. By tracking progress, people can see how far they have come and what they need to achieve goals.
- Create a support system: The book emphasizes the importance of having a support system of people who will encourage and motivate them to achieve their goal.
- Be flexible: The book encourages readers to be flexible and open to change, as it suggests that the path to achieving a goal can be unexpected and may change along the way.
- Stay focused: The book encourages readers to stay focused on their "One Thing" and not let distractions or setbacks discourage them.
- Take care of yourself: The book stresses the importance of taking care of oneself, physically, emotionally and mentally as it helps to stay focused, motivated and have the energy to achieve the goal.

CHAPTER XVII

The 80/20 Principle – Richard Koch

This book explains how the 80/20 principle, also known as the Pareto Principle, can be applied to various aspects of life in order to achieve greater efficiency and effectiveness. The principle states that 80% of effects come from 20% of causes, and can be seen in many areas such as business, finance, and personal productivity.

Koch explains how the principle can be used to identify and focus on the most important tasks, eliminate unnecessary activities, and achieve greater results with less effort. The book also covers how to apply the principle in different areas of life such as work, relationships, and health.

- Identify the vital few: Use the 80/20 principle to identify the 20% of activities that are responsible for 80% of your results and focus on them.
- Eliminate the trivial many: Identify and eliminate the 80% of activities that are only responsible for 20% of your results. This will free up time and energy to focus on the important tasks.
- Prioritize: Use the 80/20 principle to prioritize your activities by identifying which tasks are most important and which are least important.
- Delegate: Use the principle to delegate the less important tasks to others in order to free up time and energy to focus on the more important tasks.
- Look for leverage points: Use the principle to identify leverage points in your business, personal life or any other area of your life where you can make significant changes with minimal effort.
- Focus on the long-term: Use the principle to identify the activities that will have the most impact in the long-term and focus on them.
- Be selective: Use the principle to be selective about the people you spend time with, the projects you work on, and the goals you set for yourself.
- Seek balance: While the principle can be used to achieve greater efficiency, it's also important to seek balance and not neglect important aspects of your life in the pursuit of productivity.

CHAPTER XVIII

The 48 Laws of Power – Robert Greene

The book provides a historical analysis of how power has been acquired, maintained and lost throughout history, and presents 48 laws that the author argues are essential for gaining and maintaining power. The book covers a wide range of topics, including how to manipulate others, how to create an illusion of power, how to use flattery and deceit to gain advantage, and how to build a network of allies.

The book is intended as a guide for understanding the dynamics of power and how to acquire it using historic examples. The author encourages to gain knowledge from the book but use it cautiously knowing the consequences.

1. Never outshine the master: Avoid drawing too much attention to yourself and always be aware of your place in the hierarchy.
2. Never put too much trust in friends, learn how to use enemies: Keep your friends close, but your enemies closer.
3. Conceal your intentions: Keep your true intentions and plans hidden from others.
4. Always say less than necessary: Speak only when necessary and be mindful of the information you reveal.
5. So much depends on reputation—guard it with your life: Protect your reputation at all costs, as it is one of your most valuable assets.
6. Court attention at all costs: Draw attention to yourself, as visibility is key to power.
7. Get others to do the work for you, but always take the credit: Use the efforts of others to further your own goals, but make sure to take the credit for their work.
8. Make other people come to you—use bait if necessary: Control the flow of information and make others come to you for it.
9. Win through your actions, never through argument: Actions speak louder than words, use them to win others over.
10. Infection: avoid stepping into a great man's shoes: Avoid following in the footsteps of those who have already achieved great power.

CHAPTER XIX

The Power of Now – Eckhart Tolle

The book's main message is that the present moment is the only place where true happiness and fulfillment can be found, and that people often spend their lives trapped in the past or the future, missing out on the richness of the present. The book suggests that:

- The mind is often preoccupied with thoughts and worries about the past or the future, which leads to unhappiness and a sense of disconnection from the present moment.
- Practice mindfulness: Tolle encourages readers to practice mindfulness and focus on the present moment. This can be done through meditation, yoga, or other practices that help to quiet the mind and focus on the present.
- Recognize the ego: Tolle explains that the mind creates a sense of self, or an "ego" that is separate from the world around us, and that this is the root of all negative emotions such as fear, anger, and anxiety. By recognizing and identifying with the observer within ourselves, we can learn to detach from the ego and its negative thoughts and emotions.
- Cultivate gratitude and compassion: The author encourages readers to cultivate a deeper sense of gratitude and compassion towards oneself and others. This can help to shift the focus from the ego and its concerns to the present moment and to the well-being of others.
- Let go of the past and future: Tolle suggests that people often spend their lives trapped in the past or the future, missing out on the richness of the present. By letting go of the past and future, and focusing on the present, we can experience a deeper sense of peace and connection to the world around us.
- Be aware of your thoughts: Tolle encourages readers to be aware of their thoughts and not to identify with them. Thoughts come and go and it is important to observe them without getting caught up in them.
- Practice non-judgment: The author suggests to practice non-judgment towards oneself and others, this will help to release the negative emotions and thoughts, and to experience a deeper sense of peace and connection to the present moment.

CHAPTER XX

How to Win Friends and Influence People – Dale Carnegie

The book offers practical advice on how to build and maintain relationships, and how to influence and persuade others. Dale Carnegie offers a variety of tips and strategies for building and maintaining relationships, and for influencing and persuading others. The advices in the book are timeless on how to communicate effectively, build rapport, and develop positive relationships. Here are a few key tips from the book:

- Show a genuine interest in others by making them feel valued and important. This can be done by actively listening to them, asking them questions, and remembering details about their lives and interests.
- Appeal to their self-interest: To influence and persuade others, it is important to understand their perspective. This can be done by speaking in terms of the other person's interests and highlighting how your ideas or proposals will benefit them.
- Avoid criticism and complaints: Carnegie suggests that it is important to avoid arguments and criticism, and to instead focus on finding common ground and building rapport. This can be done by using "I" statements when expressing your opinions, and by avoiding blame or accusations.
- Practice active listening which means fully paying attention and understanding the other person's point of view. This can be done by repeating back what they say, paraphrasing their words, and asking follow-up questions. Carnegie stresses the importance of being a good listener, and not just talking about oneself, but being genuinely interested in others.
- Use flattery and praise effectively for building relationships and influencing others, but they must be used authentically and sincerely.
- Practice sincere apology (when one is wrong) and honest appreciation, this can help build trust and positive relationships, and will make the other person feel valued and important.

CHAPTER XXI

Think and Grow Rich – Napoleon Hill

The book teaches the reader how to think positively & overcome obstacles in order to achieve success & wealth in 13 chapters. *1st Ch. "The Riches are in the Niches,"* discusses the importance of finding one's passion & turning it into a successful business. *2nd Ch. "Desire: The Starting Point of All Achievement,"* teaches the reader that desire is the starting point of all achievement, & that one must have a burning desire for success in order to achieve it. *3rd Ch. "Faith: The Only Known Antidote for Failure,"* teaches the reader that faith is the only known antidote for failure, & that one must have faith in oneself & one's abilities in order to achieve success. *4th Ch. "Auto-Suggestion: The Medium for Influencing the Subconscious Mind,"* teaches the reader how to use auto-suggestion to influence the subconscious mind & achieve success. *5th Ch. "Specialized Knowledge: The Key to Power,"* teaches the reader that specialized knowledge is the key to power, & that one must continuously learn & improve in order to achieve success. *6th Ch. "Imagination: The Workshop of the Mind,"* teaches the reader how to use their imagination to visualize success & achieve it.

7th Ch. "Organized Planning: The Crystallization of Desire into Action," teaches the reader the importance of planning & organization in achieving success. *8th Ch. "Decision: The Master Key to Riches,"* teaches the reader that decision is the master key to riches, & that one must be decisive in order to achieve success. *9th Ch. "Persistence: The Sustained Effort Necessary to Induce Faith,"* teaches the reader that persistence is the sustained effort necessary to induce faith, & that one must persist in the face of obstacles to achieve success. *10th Ch. "Power of the Master Mind: The Driving Force,"* teaches the reader about the power of the master mind & how to harness it to achieve success. *11th Ch. "The Mystery of Sex Transmutation,"* teaches the reader about the power of sex transmutation, which is the ability to transform sexual energy into creative energy. *12th Ch. "The Subconscious Mind: The Connecting Link,"* teaches the reader about the power of the subconscious mind & how to tap into it to achieve success.

13th Ch. "The Brain: A Broadcasting & Receiving Station for Thought," teaches the reader about the power of the brain & how to use it to achieve success.

CHAPTER XXII

Rich Dad, Poor Dad – Robert Kiyosaki

The book is based on the author's experiences growing up with two "fathers" - his biological father, who was a salaried employee and struggled financially, and his "rich dad" who was a successful businessman and real estate investor. In summary, "Rich Dad, Poor Dad" argues that:

- Traditional financial education, which emphasizes saving money, investing in stocks and bonds, and working for a steady paycheck, is flawed and that it can lead to financial struggles.
- Instead, the author suggests that people should focus on building assets that generate income, such as real estate, businesses, and investments in tangible assets. This can help to create multiple streams of income and increase overall financial security.
- Financial literacy: The author encourages readers to educate themselves about money, investing, and financial markets. This can help people to make more informed financial decisions and achieve their financial goals.
- The author also stresses the importance of taking calculated risks and thinking outside of the box to achieve financial success. This can involve starting a business, investing in real estate or other unconventional investments.
- Beware of the difference between assets and liabilities, and to focus on acquiring assets that will appreciate in value over time and generate income.
- Change your mindset about money and think like an entrepreneur, and not just an employee, to achieve financial freedom.
- Create multiple streams of income: The author suggests creating multiple streams of income, as it will help to diversify and increase overall financial security.
- Don't be afraid to ask for help and to surround yourselves with people who are knowledgeable and experienced in the field they want to invest in.
- Live below your means, this way they can invest money in assets that generate income and build wealth.

CHAPTER XXIII

The Richest Man in Babylon – George S. Clason

The book is a collection of parables set in ancient Babylon that impart financial wisdom and advice on how to achieve wealth and financial success.

The Richest Man in Babylon: Arkad was once a poor scribe who was dissatisfied with his financial situation. He sought advice from the wealthiest man in Babylon, a man known as Algamish, and asked him how he had become so wealthy. Algamish told Arkad that the key to building wealth was to pay oneself first by setting aside a portion of one's income for savings and investments. He also advised Arkad to invest his money wisely and to avoid the temptations of overspending and overindebtedness.

Arkad took this advice to heart and began setting aside one-tenth of his income for savings and investments. He also sought out wise counsel from successful businessmen and investors, and learned how to invest in profitable ventures. Through hard work and discipline, Arkad was able to accumulate wealth and eventually became the richest man in Babylon, surpassing even Algamish himself. Some more parables are,

- The Seven Cures for a Lean Purse: This parable offers practical advice on how to build wealth, including living below one's means, seeking wise counsel, and investing in oneself by acquiring knowledge and skills.
- The Gold Lender of Babylon: This parable teaches the importance of being financially disciplined and the consequences of overspending and overindebtedness.
- The Five Laws of Gold: This parable offers advice on how to invest wisely, including the importance of diversifying investments and not being afraid to take calculated risks.
- The Camel Trader of Babylon: This parable teaches the importance of budgeting, being mindful of expenses and living below one's means.
- The Clay Tablets of Ur: This parable emphasizes the importance of education and financial literacy, and encourages readers to seek the advice of financially successful people.
- The Walls of Babylon: This parable encourages readers to learn from their mistakes, persevere through difficult times, and not to be afraid of failure.

CHAPTER XXIV

Money: Master the Game – Tony Robbins

he book provides a comprehensive overview of personal finance and offers practical advice on how to achieve financial freedom. The book is divided into 7 simple steps that are designed to guide readers on their journey towards financial freedom.

In summary, "Money: Master the Game" offers the following advice:

1. The first step is to take control of one's finances, this includes understanding one's current financial situation and setting clear financial goals.
2. The second step is to understand the game of money and how it works, this includes understanding the different types of investments and the role of financial advisors.
3. The third step is to learn how to invest wisely and to diversify one's investments.
4. The fourth step is to master the art of saving and budgeting, and to create a savings plan that is tailored to one's goals and lifestyle.
5. The fifth step is to learn how to manage risk and protect oneself from financial losses.
6. The sixth step is to learn how to create multiple streams of income.
7. The seventh step is to adopt the right mindset and take action towards achieving financial freedom.

Throughout the book, Robbins emphasizes the importance of taking control of one's finances, understanding the game of money, and investing wisely in order to achieve financial freedom. He also stresses the importance of creating a savings plan, managing risk, and building multiple streams of income. Additionally, the book also features exclusive interviews with some of the most successful investors in the world, such as Warren Buffett, Paul Tudor Jones, and Ray Dalio.

CHAPTER XXV

You Are a Badass at Making Money – Jen Sincero

The book focuses on helping readers change their mindset and beliefs about money, in order to manifest more wealth and success in their lives. The book covers topics such as understanding and breaking limiting beliefs, setting financial goals, and taking action to achieve them. Sincero uses personal anecdotes and examples to illustrate her points, and provides practical exercises and advice for readers to implement in their own lives.

Tips from the book are,

- Identify and challenge limiting beliefs: Sincero encourages readers to be wary of any limiting beliefs they may have about money, such as "I'll never be able to afford that" or "I'm not good with money." She suggests replacing these negative thoughts with positive affirmations, such as "I am worthy of abundance" or "I am confident in my ability to manage my finances."
- Set clear financial goals: Sincero suggests setting specific, measurable, and achievable financial goals in order to create a clear vision for what you want to achieve with your money.
- Take action: Sincero emphasizes the importance of taking action to achieve your financial goals, whether it's negotiating a raise, starting a side hustle, or investing in stocks. She stresses that simply thinking positively about money is not enough; you have to take concrete steps to make it happen.
- Create a budget: Sincero recommends creating a budget to help you understand where your money is going and make informed decisions about how to allocate it.
- Practice gratitude: Sincero encourages readers to practice gratitude for the money they already have, as a way of shifting their mindset to one of abundance and positivity.
- Keep an open mind: Sincero suggests keeping an open mind to new opportunities and ways of making money, and being willing to take risks in order to achieve financial success.

CHAPTER XXVI

Getting to Yes – Roger Fisher and William Ury

The book provides a method for negotiating effectively with various concepts and techniques viz,

- Separate the people from the problem: Try to understand the other party's perspective and avoid personalizing the negotiation.
- Focus on interests, not positions: Identify the underlying needs & concerns of both parties & try finding solutions addressing them
- Create options for mutual gain: Generate a variety of potential solutions that benefit both parties.
- Base your arguments on objective standards and facts, rather than opinions or emotions.
- Know your BATNA (best alternative to a negotiated agreement) & use it as a benchmark for any potential agreement.
- Use the "principle of least interest": Be aware of the party that has the least interest in the outcome and try to address their concerns.
- Listen actively, express yourself clearly, and be open to feedback.
- Be prepared to compromise: Be willing to make concessions in order to reach an agreement.
- Avoid making threats which escalate the situation and make it harder to reach an agreement.
- Avoid using positional bargaining (stating your position and trying to defend it), explore the other party's interests and address them.
- Focus on the present and future: Don't get bogged down in discussing past events or assigning blame. Focus on finding a solution that works for both parties moving forward.
- Keep emotions in check: Try to stay calm and avoid getting emotional during the negotiation.
- Be flexible: Be open to new ideas and be willing to change your approach if it isn't working.
- Be persistent: Don't give up if the negotiation becomes difficult. Keep working towards a solution and don't be afraid to seek help if needed.

CHAPTER XXVII

Crucial Conversations – Kerry Patterson, Joseph Grenny, Ron McMillan, and Al Switzler

The book teaches people how to handle sensitive and challenging conversations in a way that ensures a positive outcome. Here are some tips from the book:

- Start with Heart: Begin by focusing on your desired outcome and the best possible resolution.
- Learn to Look: Observe and understand the different perspectives involved in the conversation.
- Make it Safe: Create an environment in which everyone feels comfortable and free to express their opinions and feelings.
- Master My Stories: Be aware of and manage your own emotions and thoughts during the conversation.
- STATE Your Path: Communicate effectively by sharing your facts, telling your story, asking for others' paths, and exploring the differing perspectives.
- Explore Others' Paths: Seek to understand others' perspectives and motivations.
- Moving to Action: Agree on a course of action that everyone can support.
- Mutual Purpose: Focus on finding common ground and mutual purpose.
- Accountability: Ensure that everyone is held accountable for their actions and commitments.
- Learn to Look: Continuously observe the conversation and make adjustments as needed.
- Keeping Commitments: Follow through on commitments made during the conversation.
- Repair Relationships: Take steps to repair any damage to relationships caused by the conversation.
- Create a Culture of Candor: Cultivate an open, honest, and respectful culture in which crucial conversations can occur effectively.
- Show empathy and understanding towards the other person's feelings and perspectives observing the non-verbal cues with honesty.

CHAPTER XXVIII

Winning – Jack Welch

"Winning" is a valuable resource for leaders and managers looking to create a successful and high-performing organization written by the most respected CEO of GE (General Electric) Jack Welch. Some useful tips:

1. Have a clear vision and strategy: Welch emphasizes the importance of having a clear vision and strategy for the organization, and aligning all employees behind that vision.
2. Emphasize strong leadership: Welch encourages leaders to be strong and decisive, and to foster an environment of open communication and transparency.
3. Foster a culture of innovation and change: Welch encourages leaders to be willing to take risks and make bold moves in order to stay ahead of the curve and stay competitive in the market.
4. Emphasize accountability: Welch stresses the need for measurable performance metrics and a process of continuous improvement, and encourages leaders to hold all employees accountable for their actions and results.
5. Eliminate bureaucracy and inefficiencies: Welch encourages leaders to eliminate bureaucracy and inefficiencies that slow down the organization and impede progress.
6. Invest in people: Welch emphasizes the importance of investing in the development and growth of employees, and creating a culture of continuous learning and development.
7. Embrace change: Welch encourages leaders to embrace change and be adaptable to the changing business environment.
8. Encourage open communication: Welch stresses the importance of open communication and creating an environment where employees feel comfortable sharing their ideas and feedback.
9. Be passionate and committed: Welch emphasizes the importance of being passionate and committed to achieving success, and encourages leaders to lead by example.
10. Create a sense of urgency: Welch suggests creating a sense of urgency within the organization to drive progress and achieve goals.

CHAPTER XXIX

The 5 Second Rule – Mel Robbins

The book provides a simple but effective method for overcoming procrastination and taking action. The concept behind the 5 second rule is that when you have an impulse to do something, you should count down from 5 to 1 and then immediately take action. The theory is that the 5 seconds gives your brain time to process the impulse and take action, while also preventing it from being overridden by negative thoughts or doubts.

- Use the 5-second countdown: When you have an impulse to do something, count down from 5 to 1 and then immediately take action. This gives you time to process the impulse and take action before your brain can override it with negative thoughts or doubts.
- Don't overthink it: The 5-second rule is meant to be simple and easy to implement. Don't try to overthink it or make it too complicated.
- Take small actions that are easy to accomplish, such as making your bed or taking a shower. This will help you build momentum and increase your confidence.
- Be consistent: The 5-second rule works best when used consistently. Try to use it every day, even for small actions.
- Keep it positive: Use the 5-second rule to take positive actions that will help you reach your goals.
- Look for opportunities to use the 5-second rule throughout your day.
- Make it a habit: Over time, the 5-second rule can become a habit and you will find yourself taking action automatically.
- Use the 5-second rule to overcome fears and push through anxiety.
- Use it to build confidence: The more you use the 5-second rule, the more confident you will become in your ability to take action.
- Use it for your personal and professional life: The 5-second rule can be used in various aspects of life, such as personal, professional, and relationship.

Remember, the 5-second rule is a simple tool that can help you take action in the face of fear and uncertainty. The key is to be consistent and to start small, and gradually build up to bigger actions.

CHAPTER XXX

Stumbling on Happiness – Daniel Gilbert

The book explores the ways in which people attempt to predict and control their happiness, and why these attempts often fail.

1. Be mindful of the present moment: Gilbert argues that people should focus on living in the present and enjoying the little things in life.
2. Cultivate gratitude: Gilbert suggests that people should practice gratitude by being thankful for what they have, rather than always wanting more.
3. Recognize the power of the imagination: People's imagination can influence their ability to predict future happiness, so it is important to be aware of how it can lead them astray.
4. Be realistic about the future: People often overestimate how much a future event will affect their happiness, so it is important to be realistic about how much a future change will actually improve one's happiness.
5. Recognize the impact of adaptation: People have a psychological immune system that helps them adapt to change, so it is important to recognize that the initial excitement of a new event or possession will eventually fade.
6. Be open to new experiences, as they can often lead to unexpected sources of happiness.
7. Seek out social connections: Gilbert argues that social connections are an important source of happiness, so it is important to invest in relationships with friends and family.
8. Don't compare yourself to others: Gilbert suggests that people should focus on their own happiness and not compare themselves to others, as it can lead to dissatisfaction.
9. Recognize the limitations of prediction: Gilbert argues that people are not very good at predicting what will make them happy, so it is important to be open to surprises.
10. Avoid "hedonic adaptation": People tend to adjust to new circumstances and find the same level of happiness, regardless of the change. It's important to be aware of this tendency and try to find new ways to enjoy and appreciate what we already have.

CHAPTER XXXI

The Subtle Art of Not Giving a F*ck – Mark Manson

The book aims to help readers prioritize their values and focus on what truly matters in their lives. The book argues that traditional self-help books often encourage readers to focus on positive thinking and trying to be happy all the time, which is not only unrealistic but also unhealthy. Instead, Manson suggests that it is important to accept negative emotions and experiences as a natural part of life, and to focus on choosing the right problems to care about.

- Prioritize your values: Manson suggests identifying what truly matters to you in life, and focusing your energy and attention on those things.
- Be selective about what you give your attention to: Manson encourages readers to be more selective about what they give their attention and energy to, and to avoid wasting time and energy on things that don't truly matter.
- Accept negative emotions and experiences: Manson argues that it is important to accept negative emotions and experiences as a natural part of life, and to not try to suppress or avoid them.
- Choose your problems wisely: Manson suggests that it is important to choose the right problems to care about, and to not waste energy on problems that are not truly important.
- Embrace your flaws: Manson encourages readers to be honest with themselves about their flaws, accept them, and focus on how to improve themselves.
- Find purpose and meaning: Manson emphasizes that living a meaningful life is not about achieving happiness but about struggling with difficult problems, accepting and learning from failure, and finding purpose.
- Be realistic: Manson encourages readers to be realistic about what they can and cannot change, and to focus on what they can control.
- Be honest with yourself: Manson suggests being honest with yourself about your own limitations, and not to compare yourself to others, and to stop trying to please everyone.

CHAPTER XXXII

Everything Is F*cked – Mark Manson

The book is a follow-up to Manson's first book and focuses on how the human mind can create meaning and happiness despite the inherent difficulties in life.

- Accept negative thoughts and emotions as a normal part of life, and to work through them rather than trying to eliminate them.
- Develop self-awareness by understanding our own limitations and accepting our own flaws, we can find a sense of contentment and fulfillment.
- Find purpose and meaning to develop a sense of self-awareness and self-compassion - don't be hard on yourself.
- Embrace uncertainty and ambiguity as a natural part of life, and to not be afraid of change or the unknown.
- Be realistic about what they can and cannot change, and to focus on what they can control.
- Embrace the complexity of life, and not to look for simple solutions to complex problems.
- Cultivate a growth mindset, which is the idea that one's abilities and intelligence can be developed through effort and learning.
- Develop resilience, which is the ability to bounce back from difficult situations and challenges.
- Embrace vulnerability, which is the ability to be open, honest and exposed, and accepting that life is difficult and uncertain.
- Prioritize self-care, which includes taking care of physical and mental health, and taking the time to rest and recharge.
- Practice mindfulness to be present in the moment, and aware of one's thoughts and emotions.
- Develop strong relationships with family, friends, and loved ones for your emotional well-being.
- Seek help when needed, whether it is therapy, counseling or support groups, and to not be afraid to ask for help.
- Be open to change and to be willing to try new things, and to be willing to change one's perspective and beliefs if necessary.

CHAPTER XXXIII

Mastery – Robert Greene

The book provides a comprehensive guide to achieving mastery in any field of work or study. The book presents the idea that mastery is not something that comes naturally but it is the result of a long-term dedication, hard work and a process of learning and developing. The book also argues that true mastery is not about achieving a single goal, but about a lifelong process of learning, growing and self-improvement.

Here are some tips from "Mastery" on how to achieve mastery in any field:

1. Find your life's task: Greene suggests that people should find their life's task, the work that they are most passionate about and that aligns with their natural talents.
2. Develop a beginner's mind: Approach your work with curiosity, openness and a willingness to learn, this will help you to see things in a new light and make new connections.
3. Build a solid foundation: Learn the basics of your field thoroughly, this will provide a solid foundation for further learning and development.
4. Learn from the masters: Seek out mentors and learn from the best in your field, this will provide you with valuable knowledge and skills.
5. Practice deliberately: Practice your skills in a focused and deliberate way, this will help you to improve quickly and achieve mastery.
6. Embrace failure: Failure is an inevitable part of the learning process, embrace it and learn from it.
7. Experiment and take risks: Experiment with new ideas and take risks, this will help you to find new solutions and achieve breakthroughs.
8. Stay curious and keep learning: Mastery is a lifelong process, so stay curious and keep learning, this will help you to continue to grow and improve.
9. Be patient: Mastery takes time and patience, so don't be discouraged by setbacks or delays.
10. Have a sense of purpose: Have a sense of purpose, this will keep you motivated and focused on your goals, even when the going gets tough.

CHAPTER XXXIV

Mindset – Carol Dweck

The book explores the idea of a "growth mindset," which is the belief that one's abilities and intelligence can be developed through hard work and effort. Dweck argues that a growth mindset can lead to greater success and satisfaction in life, while a "fixed mindset" - the belief that one's abilities are set in stone - can hold individuals back.

Some tips for developing a growth mindset include:

- Embracing challenges and viewing them as opportunities for growth
- Learning from mistakes and failures
- Emphasizing the process of learning and growth, rather than just the end result
- Cultivating a love of learning and seeking out new experiences
- Embracing feedback and using it to improve.
- Being open to new ideas and perspectives
- Recognizing that intelligence and abilities are not fixed, but can be developed through effort
- Focusing on effort and progress, not just innate talent or ability
- Being persistent and not giving up easily
- Surrounding yourself with people who have a growth mindset and who will support and encourage your efforts.

Additionally, Dweck suggests that parents, teachers, and coaches can foster a growth mindset in children and students by praising them for their effort, helping them to see the value in learning from mistakes and setbacks, and encouraging them to take on new challenges.

Dweck tells the story of a fifth-grade student named Michael. Michael was a hardworking student, but he struggled with math. His teacher, Mrs. Wilson, noticed this and decided to try a new approach. Instead of praising Michael for his intelligence or innate ability, she praised him for his effort and progress. She told him that she could see he was working hard and that he was improving. Michael began to change his attitude towards math eventually getting better at math.

CHAPTER XXXV

Outliers – Malcolm Gladwell

In the book, Gladwell argues that success is not solely determined by individual talent or intelligence, but also by a combination of factors such as cultural background, family, and opportunities. He uses examples from various fields, including sports, music, and technology, to support his argument. Some key takeaways from the book include:

1. Embrace your cultural background that has shaped you and use it to your advantage by understanding the norms and values to give you a unique perspective which'll help you stand out in your field.
2. Seek out opportunities that will help you advance in your field. This could include internships, networking events, or taking on additional responsibilities at work.
3. Surround yourself with successful people - mentors and role models who have achieved success in your field. Not only can they provide guidance and support, but they can also open doors.
4. Be persistent: Don't give up on your goals, even when faced with setbacks or obstacles.
5. Recognize that learning and growth are ongoing processes. Embrace a growth mindset..
6. Understand that success is often a combination of hard work, talent, and opportunity. Recognize that luck also plays a role in shaping our success, and do your best.
7. Practice, practice, practice: Gladwell's 10,000 hours rule highlights the importance of practice in achieving expertise. Identify the areas and make practice a priority.
8. Embrace diversity in all its forms, and seek out individuals and perspectives that are different from your own. This can help you learn new skills and expand your understanding of the world.
9. Take risks: Be willing to step outside your comfort zone and try new things. The more risks you take, the more opportunities you will have to learn and grow.
10. Be adaptable: Recognize that the world is constantly changing, and stay open to new ideas and be willing to change course when necessary.

CHAPTER XXXVI

Declutter Your Mind – S. J. Scott

The book aims to help readers declutter their minds from negative thoughts, worries, and anxieties that prevent them from achieving their goals and living a more fulfilling life.

Some key takeaways from the book include:

1. Recognize the source of your negative thoughts: Identify the source of your negative thoughts, whether it be past experiences, external influences, or internal beliefs, and work on addressing them.
2. Reframe your thoughts: Learn to reframe your negative thoughts into positive ones by focusing on the present moment and the things you are grateful for.
3. Practice mindfulness: Mindfulness practices such as meditation, yoga, or journaling can help you become more aware of your thoughts and emotions, and can help you detach from them.
4. Develop a self-care routine: A self-care routine that includes healthy habits such as exercise, proper nutrition, and enough sleep can help improve your mental and physical well-being.
5. Prioritize your time: Declutter your schedule by focusing on what's important and eliminating activities that don't add value to your life.
6. Learn to let go: Let go of negative thoughts and emotions that no longer serve you, and don't hold on to things that you cannot change.
7. Create a vision board: Creating a vision board with pictures and quotes that represent your goals and aspirations can help you stay motivated and focused on what you want to achieve.
8. Surround yourself with positive people: The people you surround yourself with have a big impact on your mental state, so make sure to surround yourself with positive people.
9. Stay organized: Keeping your physical space organized can have a positive impact on your mental state. Try to declutter your living space and keep it tidy.
10. Practice gratitude: Incorporating gratitude practices into your daily routine can help you focus on the positive aspects of your life, and can help reduce stress and anxiety.

CHAPTER XXXVII

No Excuses! – Brian Tracy

In his book "No Excuses: The Power of Self-Discipline", Brian Tracy argues that success is primarily determined by self-discipline and the ability to take consistent action towards one's goals. Tracy asserts that successful individuals possess key traits such as focus, persistence, and the ability to overcome obstacles and temptations. He provides practical tips and strategies for developing self-discipline, including setting clear goals, creating a supportive environment, and developing positive habits. The book aims to inspire readers to take control of their lives, overcome their excuses, and achieve their full potential.

- Set clear, specific and measurable goals: Identify what you want to achieve and have a plan for how to get there.
- Focus on results: Avoid distractions and stay focused on what is important.
- Take action every day: Consistent, small steps lead to progress.
- Overcome procrastination: Tackle tasks immediately, avoid delays and prioritize important tasks.
- Develop positive habits: Habits shape your life, form good habits and break bad ones.
- Build self-discipline muscles: Like a muscle, self-discipline can be strengthened with practice.
- Stay motivated: Find meaning and purpose in your work, and stay inspired.
- Eliminate negative self-talk: Replace negative thoughts with positive affirmations and visualization.
- Learn from failures: Use failures as opportunities to learn and grow.
- Surround yourself with support: Seek out supportive friends, family, and mentors to help you succeed.
- Stay organized: Keep your environment and schedule organized for greater productivity.
- Celebrate small victories: Acknowledge your successes, no matter how small, to maintain motivation.

CHAPTER XXXVIII

Eat that frog! – Brian Tracy

"Eat That Frog!" is a book written by Brian Tracy that advocates for tackling the most important and difficult task first thing in the morning, or "eating the frog," to increase productivity and decrease procrastination.

Author describes the tasks to be done everyday as frogs. Start your day with eating the ugliest frog i.e, start with the most difficult one in the morning. Before you realize the day would have become already productive.

Key tips from the book include:

- Prioritize tasks based on importance and urgency
- Focus on one task at a time
- Set specific, measurable and achievable goals
- Use the 80/20 rule (focus on 20% of activities that produce 80% of results)
- Break down large tasks into smaller, manageable steps
- Minimize distractions and stay focused
- Use time-management techniques like time blocking, delegating, and saying "no" to non-essential tasks.
- Celebrate small wins and reward yourself for completing tasks.
- Learn to say "No" to distractions, requests and time-wasters
- Use visualization to stay motivated and focused on your goals
- Take regular breaks to recharge and maintain focus
- Surround yourself with positive and productive people
- Keep learning and developing new skills to stay ahead
- Focus on outcomes, not just activity
- Use deadlines to increase your motivation and accountability
- Minimize non-essential activities and simplify your life.
- Use positive self-talk and affirmations to maintain confidence and motivation.

CHAPTER XXXIX

Tools of Titans – Timothy Ferriss

"Tools of Titans" is a book by Timothy Ferriss that shares insights and lessons from over 200 of the world's top performers across a variety of fields, including business, sports, and entertainment.

Key takeaways from the book include:

- Embrace stoicism to maintain mental resilience and remain calm under stress.
- Cultivate a strong morning routine to set the tone for the day.
- Focus on results, not just activity.
- Embrace experimentation and embrace failure as a learning opportunity.
- Build healthy habits and prioritize self-care for optimal performance.
- Seek out mentors and surround yourself with successful, growth-oriented individuals.
- Optimize your nutrition and diet for peak performance.
- Minimize distractions and focus on what truly matters.
- Continuously learn, grow, and adapt to stay ahead.
- Cultivate a strong sense of purpose and take meaningful action towards your goals.
- Practice mindfulness and meditation to improve focus, clarity, and well-being.
- Adopt a growth mindset and view challenges and failures as opportunities for growth.
- Prioritize sleep for better physical and mental health.
- Create a supportive environment that enables you to achieve your goals.
- Continuously evaluate and adjust your priorities to align with your goals.
- Use positive visualization to clarify and reinforce your goals.
- Focus on strengths and delegate or outsource weaknesses.
- Maintain a positive outlook and cultivate a growth-oriented mindset.
- Experiment and try new things to continuously learn and grow.
- Take consistent, deliberate, and meaningful action towards your goals.

CHAPTER XL

Failing Forward – John C. Maxwell

"Failing Forward" is a book by John C. Maxwell that explores the importance of failure and its role in success.

Here are the key tips and strategies from the book:

- Embrace failure as an opportunity for growth and learning.
- Learn from your failures and use them to improve your skills and knowledge.
- Reframe failures as temporary setbacks, not permanent failures.
- Focus on the positives and find the benefits in each failure.
- Develop resilience and persistence to overcome challenges and adversity.
- Seek feedback and use it to continuously improve and evolve.
- Take responsibility for your failures and use them as a catalyst for change.
- Surround yourself with supportive people who encourage and motivate you.
- Set realistic goals and expectations to avoid becoming discouraged.
- Don't be afraid to take risks and pursue your passions, even if they come with the risk of failure.

Here's an anecdote from the book: John C. Maxwell shares the story of Thomas Edison, who failed over a thousand times before finally inventing the successful light bulb. Instead of becoming discouraged, Edison reframed his failures as learning opportunities and used them to continuously improve and refine his invention.

The anecdote highlights the importance of persistence and resilience, and serves as a reminder that failure is a normal and necessary part of the journey to success.

CHAPTER XLI

Radical Acceptance – Tara Brach

"Radical Acceptance: Embracing Your Life with the Heart of a Buddha" by Tara Brach is a book that explores the concept of radical acceptance, which is the practice of fully accepting and embracing one's life experiences, both positive and negative, without judgment. The book teaches readers how to cultivate self-awareness and compassion, and how to live a life of greater peace and well-being. Here are some tips from the book:

- Practice mindfulness: Cultivate awareness of your thoughts, emotions, and experiences in the present moment.
- Embrace your emotions: Allow yourself to fully experience and accept your emotions, without judgment or resistance.
- Cultivate self-compassion: Treat yourself with kindness and understanding, as you would with a dear friend.
- Let go of judgment: Release judgment of yourself and others, and cultivate a non-judgmental attitude.
- Practice self-acceptance: Embrace all aspects of yourself, including your strengths and weaknesses.
- Connect with your values: Clarify your values and live in alignment with them.
- Cultivate gratitude: Practice gratitude by acknowledging the good in your life.
- Seek support: Seek out supportive relationships to help you in your journey.
- Embrace impermanence: Accept the reality that all things are constantly changing, and that nothing lasts forever.
- Live in the present moment: Focus on the here and now, and let go of worries about the future or regrets about the past.

Anecdote: In the book, Tara Brach shares her own personal experience of overcoming anxiety and depression through the practice of radical acceptance. She shares how, through mindfulness and self-compassion, she was able to accept and embrace her emotions, thoughts, and experiences, and move towards a life of greater peace and well-being.

CHAPTER XLII

Stillness Is the Key – Ryan Holiday

"Stillness is the Key" is a book by Ryan Holiday that explores the concept of stillness and its role in leadership, creativity, and success.

Key takeaways from the book include:

- Embrace stillness to increase focus, creativity, and success.
- Reduce distractions and simplify your life to find peace and clarity.
- Cultivate mindfulness and presence to increase awareness and well-being.
- Practice deliberate and mindful decision-making to improve outcomes.
- Develop a strong sense of self-awareness to better understand your motivations and goals.
- Cultivate resilience and grit to persevere through challenges and adversity.
- Find meaning and purpose in your work to increase motivation and satisfaction.
- Invest in personal growth and development to continuously improve and evolve.
- Embrace simplicity and minimize clutter to increase clarity and focus.
- Cultivate inner peace and stillness to reduce stress and increase happiness.

Here's an anecdote from the book:

Ryan Holiday shares the story of a young, successful CEO named Dan, who had achieved everything he wanted in life, but felt unfulfilled and stressed. Despite his success, Dan felt like he was constantly chasing something and never truly finding happiness. Ryan introduced Dan to the concept of stillness and encouraged him to focus on simplifying his life, reducing distractions, and embracing mindfulness and presence. Over time, Dan began to feel more relaxed and content, and was able to find more joy and satisfaction in his work and personal life. The anecdote serves as a reminder that success and material wealth do not necessarily equal happiness, and that cultivating stillness and simplifying our lives can lead to increased well-being and contentment.

CHAPTER XLIII

Tiny Beautiful Things – Cheryl Strayed

"Tiny Beautiful Things: Advice on Love and Life from Dear Sugar" by Cheryl Strayed is a collection of advice columns written by the author under the pseudonym "Dear Sugar". The book offers advice and support on various topics, including relationships, heartbreak, loss, and personal growth.

Here are some tips from the book:

- Embrace vulnerability: Being vulnerable allows for deeper connections and growth.
- Let go of shame: Stop holding on to shame and embrace your true self.
- Practice self-compassion: Treat yourself with the same kindness and understanding that you show to others.
- Let go of expectations: Embrace the present moment and release expectations for how things should be.
- Be honest: Honesty builds trust and creates deeper relationships.
- Seek support: Seek out the support of loved ones when going through difficult times.
- Take risks: Taking risks leads to growth and self-discovery.
- Embrace change: Change is inevitable, embrace it and grow from it.
- Practice forgiveness: Forgive yourself and others for mistakes and let go of resentment.
- Be kind: Show kindness and compassion to those around you, even in the face of adversity.
- Live in the present moment: Focus on the here and now, and let go of worries about the future or regrets about the past.
- Cultivate gratitude: Practice gratitude by acknowledging the good in your life, no matter how small.
- Embrace uncertainty: Embrace the unknown and understand that it is a normal part of life.
- Empower others: Empower those around you by showing them love and support.
- Be authentic: Be true to yourself and live a life that aligns with your values and beliefs.

CHAPTER XLIV

Eat Pray Love – Elizabeth Gilbert

"Eat Pray Love" is a memoir by Elizabeth Gilbert that recounts her journey of self-discovery and personal growth, as she travels through Italy, India, and Indonesia.

Key takeaways from the book include:

1. Embrace change and uncertainty as opportunities for growth and discovery.
2. Practice self-care and self-love to nurture personal well-being.
3. Seek fulfillment and inner peace through spiritual practices, such as meditation and prayer.
4. Cultivate gratitude and mindfulness to appreciate life's simple pleasures.
5. Let go of societal expectations and embrace your true self.
6. Seek balance in all aspects of life: work, love, and spirituality.
7. Seek meaningful connections and relationships with others.
8. Take risks, pursue passions and live life with purpose.
9. Find joy and happiness in the present moment, and don't dwell on past mistakes or future fears.
10. Trust in the universe and have faith in the journey of life.

Summary: "Eat Pray Love" is a personal journey of self-discovery and growth, as the author travels through Italy, India, and Indonesia seeking fulfillment and inner peace. The book encourages readers to embrace change, practice self-care, seek balance and purpose in life, and cultivate gratitude and mindfulness.

CHAPTER XLV

The 5 Love Languages – Gary Chapman

"The 5 Love Languages" is a book by Gary Chapman that explores the different ways people express and receive love.

Here are the key tips and strategies from the book:

- Identify your primary love language and understand how you express and receive love.
- Learn your partner's love language and use it to communicate and strengthen your relationship.
- Express love and affection in ways that are meaningful to your partner.
- Pay attention to non-verbal cues and gestures, such as touch and eye contact.
- Make time for quality time and shared experiences with your partner.
- Show appreciation and gratitude for the love and support your partner provides.
- Be intentional and consistent in expressing love and affection.
- Seek to understand and respect your partner's love language, even if it is different from your own.
- Forgive easily and communicate openly and honestly to resolve conflicts and misunderstandings.
- Invest time and effort into maintaining and strengthening your relationship.

The 5 love languages are:

Words of Affirmation | Acts of Service | Receiving Gifts | Physical Touch | Quality Time.

Here's an anecdote from the book: Gary Chapman shares the story of a couple who were experiencing conflict and communication problems in their relationship. By identifying and understanding their love languages, they were able to improve their communication and strengthen their bond. The story highlights the importance of being intentional and proactive in expressing and receiving love in a way that is meaningful to both partners.

CHAPTER XLVI

The Happiness Advantage – Shawn Achor

"The Happiness Advantage" is a book by Shawn Achor that explores the connection between happiness and success, and argues that happiness should be seen as a cause, not a result, of success.

Key takeaways from the book include:

- Cultivate a positive mindset to improve performance and resilience.
- Practice gratitude to increase happiness and well-being.
- Exercise regularly to boost mood and productivity.
- Foster strong social connections to increase happiness and reduce stress.
- Practice mindfulness and meditation to reduce stress and increase focus.
- Set achievable goals and find meaning and purpose in work.
- Embrace challenges as opportunities for growth and learning.
- Foster a positive work environment to increase job satisfaction and performance.
- Practice random acts of kindness to increase happiness and well-being.
- Reframe negative thoughts and challenges as opportunities for growth.
- Focus on your strengths to increase confidence and well-being.
- Engage in activities that bring you joy and fulfillment.
- Invest in personal and professional development to increase skills and success.
- Seek out new experiences and challenges to broaden your perspective and increase happiness.
- Prioritize self-care and take time for yourself to recharge and reduce stress.
- Surround yourself with positive and supportive people.
- Practice positive self-talk and reframe negative thoughts.
- Find humor and laughter in daily life to boost happiness and reduce stress.
- Find a healthy balance between work and personal life.
- Embrace change and uncertainty as opportunities for growth and discovery.

CHAPTER XLVII

Talk Like TED – Carmine Gallo

"Talk Like TED" is a book by Carmine Gallo that explores the strategies and techniques used by successful TED speakers to captivate and inspire audiences.

Here are the key tips and strategies from the book:

1. Start with a powerful opening that hooks the audience and sets the tone for your talk.
2. Use storytelling to make your ideas more relatable and memorable.
3. Use analogies, metaphors, and vivid imagery to help audiences understand complex ideas.
4. Show, don't tell. Use visuals and demonstrations to bring your ideas to life.
5. Emphasize the importance and impact of your ideas to inspire action.
6. Use humor, surprises, and other techniques to keep the audience engaged and entertained.
7. Convey your message with passion, conviction, and authenticity.
8. Use body language and vocal variety to reinforce your message and build rapport with the audience.
9. End with a memorable conclusion that leaves a lasting impact.
10. Practice and rehearse your talk to ensure delivery with confidence and charisma.

Here's an anecdote from the book: Carmine Gallo shares the story of a scientist named Dr. Hans Rosling, who delivered a TED talk on global health trends. Dr. Rosling used visuals, storytelling, and humor to engage the audience and make complex data more accessible and memorable.

His talk received widespread acclaim, and he became known for his ability to communicate complex ideas in a captivating and inspiring way. The anecdote demonstrates the power of storytelling and effective communication, and how incorporating these techniques can make your ideas more impactful and memorable.

CHAPTER XLVIII

Create or Hate – Dan Norris

"Create or Hate" is a book by Dan Norris, a startup entrepreneur, and marketer. The book provides a practical guide to creating a successful business and offers tips for building a successful company culture. The book emphasizes the importance of being creative and taking action to build a successful business.

Here are some tips from the book:

- Focus on creating value: Make sure that the products and services you offer bring real value to your customers.
- Be agile: Be flexible and adaptable to changing market conditions and customer needs.
- Prioritize creativity: Encourage creativity and innovation in your business to stay ahead of the competition.
- Embrace risk-taking: Be willing to take calculated risks to drive growth and success.
- Build a strong culture: Foster a supportive and collaborative company culture to engage employees and drive success.
- Hire the right people: Choose your team wisely and hire individuals who align with your values and goals.
- Invest in marketing: Make sure that your marketing strategies reach and engage your target audience.
- Focus on your customer: Make your customer the center of your business and always strive to meet their needs.
- Embrace transparency: Be open and honest with your customers and employees to build trust.
- Take action: Take consistent and focused action to achieve your goals and drive success.
- Measure success: Regularly measure your success and adjust your strategies as needed to continue to grow.
- Stay motivated: Stay motivated and focused on your goals, even when faced with challenges and setbacks.

CHAPTER XLIX

Steal Like an Artist – Austin Kleon

"Steal Like an Artist" is a book by Austin Kleon that explores the art of creativity and how to cultivate it.

Here are the key tips and strategies from the book:

- Embrace your influences and be inspired by the work of others.
- Don't be afraid to "steal" ideas and techniques from other artists and make them your own.
- Be curious and keep learning to expand your creativity.
- Keep a notebook or journal to capture your ideas and thoughts.
- Limit your distractions and focus on your work.
- Experiment and try new things to find your own unique style.
- Take breaks and step away from your work to avoid burnout.
- Surround yourself with other artists and creatives to exchange ideas and collaborate.
- Share your work with others and seek feedback to grow and improve.
- Have faith in yourself and your creativity, and keep creating even if you don't see immediate results.

Here's an anecdote from the book: Austin Kleon shares the story of Pablo Picasso, who once said, "good artists borrow, great artists steal." The anecdote highlights the importance of embracing your influences and using them to inspire your own work. By being open to new ideas and techniques, and making them your own, you can cultivate your creativity and find your own unique style.

CHAPTER L

Sleep Smarter – Shawn Stevenson

The book provides tips and strategies for improving sleep quality and achieving better health, productivity, and success. Here are the 21 tips from the book:

1. Prioritize sleep and ensure you get 7-9 hours of sleep per night.
2. Establish a routine to improve the quality of your sleep.
3. Avoid caffeine and alcohol before bedtime as they can interfere with sleep.
4. Exercise regularly to enhance physical and mental health.
5. Use natural light during the day and minimize exposure to screens before bedtime.
6. Manage stress through exercise, meditation, or deep breathing.
7. Create a sleep-friendly environment: cool, quiet, and dark.
8. Limit napping during the day and avoid taking long naps close to bedtime.
9. Use aromatherapy with essential oils into your sleep routine to relax.
10. If necessary, consider using natural sleep aids, such as melatonin.
11. Sleeping on your back can reduce the risk of sleep apnea and other breathing issues.
12. Maintain a healthy diet that includes fruits, vegetables, & proteins.
13. Reduce screen time before bedtime to minimize the impact of blue light on sleep patterns.
14. Get moving: engage in physical activity during the day.
15. Maintain a sleep journal to track your sleep habits and identify patterns.
16. Seek professional help of a sleep specialist to diagnose and treat any sleep-related issues.
17. Practice relaxation techniques such as meditation or yoga.
18. Make sleep a priority and ensure that you get enough sleep each night.
19. Avoid late-night snacking as this can interfere with sleep.
20. Experiment with different sleep strategies and habits to find what works best for you.
21. Stay committed to improving your sleep habits for optimal health, productivity, and success.

Conclusion

In conclusion, this book offers a comprehensive overview of some of the most influential self-help books of our time. By distilling the essential messages of these books into concise summaries, the book provides a powerful resource for anyone seeking to improve their life and achieve their goals. From the importance of mindfulness and self-reflection in "The Happiness Advantage" to the power of positive thinking in "The Power of Positive Thinking" and the impact of love languages in "The 5 Love Languages", the books covered in this summary offer a range of approaches to self-improvement.

Ultimately, the key to success with these self-help books is to find the ideas and strategies that resonate with you, and to be willing to put them into practice. Whether you are looking to boost your confidence, improve your relationships, or find more happiness and fulfillment in life, there is something in this book for everyone. By reading and applying the insights from these books, you can take a big step towards creating the life you want and achieving your full potential.

I recommend reading this book frequently - revisit the tips and strategies, mull over it, and reflect: if you resonate deeply, go for the full book. Reading this book continuously, you might find many books astoundingly similar - that's because they are selected in the same category. Find the path or set of books that shows you the light.

www.ingramcontent.com/pod-product-compliance
Lightning Source LLC
Chambersburg PA
CBHW020510160726
47991CB00007B/2894